EXPECTING

A CHILD IS BORN

BY: DR. RANDY T. JOHNSON
& PASTOR ROY TOWNSEND

WITH CONTRIBUTIONS FROM:

NOBLE BAIRD	MICHAEL FOX	PHILIP PIASECKI
JOHN CARTER	KENNY HOVIS	JEREMY SMITH
SIERRA COMBS	SHAWNA JOHNSON	RYAN STORY
ANGELA COX	DEBBIE KERR	KYLE WENDEL
BRYAN FOX	JOANNA MONTGOMERY	GARY WRIGHT
DONNA FOX	JILL OSMON	JEANNIE YATES

DESIGNED BY LORENA HABER
FORMATTED BY SHAWNA JOHNSON

Expecting: A Child is Born

Copyright © 2023 by The River Church

Published by The River Church
    8393 E. Holly Rd.
    Holly, MI 48442

No part of this book may be reproduced or transmitted in any form or by any means, electronic or mechanical, including photocopying, recording or by any information storage and retrieval system, without the written permission of The River Church. Inquiries should be sent to the publisher. All rights reserved.

Second Edition, December 2023

Printed in the United States of America

Scripture quotations are from the ESV® Bible (The Holy Bible, English Standard Version®), copyright © 2001 by Crossway, a publishing ministry of Good News Publishers. Used by permission. All rights reserved. The ESV text may not be quoted in any publication made available to the public by a Creative Commons license. The ESV may not be translated in whole or in part into any other language. The Holy Bible, English Standard Version®, is adapted from the Revised Standard Version of the Bible, copyright Division of Christian Education of the National Council of the Churches of Christ in the U.S.A.

1. Wonderful Counselor

- 9   Study Guide
- 19   Devotion #1: Releasing Control to the Wonderful Counselor
- 21   Devotion #2: Courtroom of Life
- 23   Devotion #3: God's Job Description
- 25   Devotion #4: Know it All
- 27   Devotion #5: Wonderful Christmastime
- 29   Devotion #6: Letters to My Little Ones

2. Mighty God

- 33   Study Guide
- 41   Devotion #1: Having Complete Power
- 43   Devotion #2: Letters to My Little Ones
- 45   Devotion #3: El Gibbor
- 47   Devotion #4: My Hero
- 49   Devotion #5: How Mighty Is Your God?
- 51   Devotion #6: Mighty to Save

3. Everlasting Father

- 55   Study Guide
- 63   Devotion #1: Gobstopper
- 65   Devotion #2: Never Leave Nor Forsake
- 67   Devotion #3: Willy Wonka
- 69   Devotion #4: The Child Is the Everlasting Father
- 71   Devotion #5: Letters to My Little Ones
- 73   Devotion #6: Compassion

4. Prince of Peace

- 77   Study Guide
- 87   Devotion #1: Jordan
- 89   Devotion #2: A Peaceful Season
- 91   Devotion #3: *"It Is Well with My Soul"*
- 95   Devotion #4: Letters to My Little Ones
- 97   Devotion #5: Endless
- 99   Devotion #6: Peace and Glory

5. Isaiah 9:1-7

- 103   Scripture Reading
- 107   Devotion #1: Worth the Wait
- 109   Devotion #2: Kingdom Building
- 111   Devotion #3: Politics
- 113   Devotion #4: Peace and Order
- 115   Devotion #5: He Is Faithful
- 117   Devotion #6: Chaos at Christmas

Preface

"For to us a child is born, to us a son is given; and the government shall be upon his shoulder, and his name shall be called Wonderful Counselor, Mighty God, Everlasting Father, Prince of Peace." Isaiah 9:6

"There are two hundred and fifty-six names given in the Bible for the Lord Jesus Christ, and I suppose this was because He was infinitely beyond all that any one name could express." Billy Sunday

Wonderful Counselor

Dr. Randy T. Johnson

I enjoy watching the television show *"Shark Tank."* One of the "sharks" has given himself the nickname "Mr. Wonderful." Self-imposed nicknames do not count, and it is clear from his co-hosts that he is not viewed that way by them.

1. What nicknames have you had?
___
___
___

One of the names given of the Messiah (Jesus) is ***"Wonderful Counselor."*** Isaiah 9:6 says, ***"For to us a child is born, to us a son is given; and the government shall be upon his shoulder, and his name shall be called Wonderful Counselor, Mighty God, Everlasting Father, Prince of Peace."***

Jesus was and is wonderful. He is extraordinary, exceptional, and distinguished. Scripture records numerous times of Him being miraculous. He gave sight to the blind, the lame walked, and He even raised the dead back to life. He is the real "Mr. Wonderful."

Years before Isaiah called the Messiah the ***"Wonderful Counselor,"*** Jesus appeared as ***"the angel of the Lord"*** to Samson's dad, Manoah. Judges 13:18 records an insightful conversation, ***"And the angel of the Lord said to him, 'Why do you ask my name, seeing it is wonderful?'"*** Whether you call Him the Messiah, the angel of the Lord, or Jesus; He is wonderful!

2. What is a "Christophany"?
___
___
___

Jesus has existed forever, and He appeared at times even before He was "born." That is amazing, awesome, and wonderful.

He not only possesses the trait of being wonderful, but His skill combines with His skill of counseling. He gives wise advice, helps those contemplating as they make plans, and gives counsel. We need to listen to this authoritative One. He knows the future and what is best for us. He is the *"Wonderful Counselor."*

3. What thoughts come to mind when you think of Jesus as the *"Wonderful Counselor"*?

___
___
___

One of the best scenarios I obtained through my counseling classes, was to ask three questions.

What is the problem?

The first question sounds pretty basic, "What is the problem?" However, it often is not what the individual thinks. A person struggling with depression might be able to help their emotional well-being through routine exercise, a proper diet, and some sound sleep (I am not saying this will solve all depression, and I am not anti-medication). They are saying the problem is depression, but it is really life choices.

4. What are some examples where you have heard someone describe their problem, but you know it has deeper roots?

___
___
___

The Bible describes man's biggest problem – sin. Romans 3:23 says, *"For all have sinned and fall short of the glory of God."* Not only is sin the problem, but it gets worse. Romans 6:23 adds, *"For the wages of sin is death, but the free gift of God is eternal life in Christ Jesus our Lord."* Sin is the problem, and it leads to death, Hell, and the Lake of Fire. Fortunately, *"Christ Jesus our*

Lord" is the ***"Wonderful Counselor."*** He not only revealed the problem, but He also provided the solution in Himself. Romans 5:8 says, ***"But God shows his love for us in that while we were still sinners, Christ died for us."*** Jesus not only knows the cure; He is the cure. He died for us. Finally, Romans 10:13 says, ***"For everyone who calls on the name of the Lord will be saved."*** Salvation comes from Jesus alone!

Charles Spurgeon said it so well, "I have a great need for Christ; I have a great Christ for my need."

- The problem might appear as a poor self-image; the cure is found in Jesus.
- The problem might appear as fear; the cure is found in Jesus.
- The problem might appear as anger or hatred; the cure is found in Jesus.
- The problem does not matter as much as the cure is the ***"Wonderful Counselor."***

5. What struggle have you had that the ***"Wonderful Counselor"*** cured?

_____
_____
_____

What have you done about it?

I used to ask about the problem and then immediately tried to solve it. I have learned that there are times when my wife or children just need support and a sounding board. It is not much different from a counselor. I am learning not to immediately jump in with advice.

This second question is so important, "What have you done about it?" They need to take some ownership of their life and growth.

Philippians 4:13 says, *"I can do all things through him who strengthens me."* Paul boldly states that he can be victorious in life through the power of Jesus Christ. This is true of all believers. If they have given their lives to Jesus, then the Holy Spirit dwells within them. They can move from victim to victorious!

6. Do you tend to immediately try to solve the problems of others?

___
___
___

7. How can it be wrong for us to immediately try to be the solution to someone else's problem?

___
___
___

David knew his spiritual, physical, and emotional strength came from the Lord. He wrote in Psalm 16:7 saying, *"I bless the Lord who gives me counsel; in the night also my heart instructs me."* David needed direction, and He found it in the Lord.

8. Where do you first go when you need counseling?

___
___
___

David found counsel in the Lord. His son, Solomon, also knew He wanted the wisdom and counsel that only God could supply. He wrote in Proverbs 8:14, *"I have counsel and sound wisdom; I have insight; I have strength."* I love the confidence that jumps off the page as he boldly proclaims what he has in the Lord.

James 1:5 says, *"If any of you lacks wisdom, let him ask God, who gives generously to all without reproach, and it will be given him."*

9. What does this passage say about counseling?

_____
_____
_____

10. What is promised in this passage?

_____
_____
_____

Finally, Romans 11:33-34 reminds us of what we have in Jesus, **"Oh, the depth of the riches and wisdom and knowledge of God! How unsearchable are his judgments and how inscrutable his ways! 'For who has known the mind of the Lord, or who has been his counselor?'"**

What do you need from me?

After we decipher what the actual problem is and we empower them in the Lord, then it is time for us to find out how we fit into the solution. Scripture does not reprimand people for seeking counsel from others.

Proverbs 15:22 says, **"Without counsel plans fail, but with many advisers they succeed."** It is wise to approach wise counsel from those who live in righteousness.

11. How can others help us in counseling?

_____
_____
_____

As counselors, we need to remember that our main objective is to point people to the Lord. Colossians 2:3 reminds us Jesus is the treasure chest, **"In whom are hidden all the treasures of wisdom and knowledge."**

12. How can we help others in counseling?

_____
_____
_____

Jesus is the *"Wonderful Counselor."* Isaiah stated it in Isaiah 9:6 and reiterated it later, *"This also comes from the Lord of hosts; he is wonderful in counsel and excellent in wisdom"* (Isaiah 28:29).

13. Knowing Jesus is the *"Wonderful Counselor,"* how should that affect our lives?

_____
_____
_____

"You don't realize Jesus is all you need until Jesus is all you have."
Tim Keller

Notes

Releasing Control to the Wonderful Counselor

Devotion #1 - Joanna Montgomery

I like to think of myself as easygoing, not afraid of change, and flexible in dealing with situations; but in truth, I am not. Whether my teenager is learning to drive, or I am supposed to delegate jobs to others, I struggle not to take matters into my own hands. The more I am invested in a situation, the more control I want to take.

Waiting is one of life's greatest challenges, and taking control and rushing God's perfectly timed steps throws us out of sync with His will. God will accomplish His purposes with or without us, but in our desire to control we miss the blessing of partnering with Him in His great work. I love Psalm 46:10, **"Be still, and know that I am God**." It sounds pretty easy for about two minutes and thirty seconds. However, after that, I am expecting God to reveal my path! (Yup, I even want to control God. Ugh!)

I want to be in control so everything will turn out the way I envisioned, and nothing will get messed up. (This is only in my head because when I handle things on my own, I often make a mess.) I am thankful when I face challenges so I know I am not alone. I have a Wonderful Counselor to guide and direct me and teach me that I am not sufficient - if I will seek Him.

Christ is our Wonderful Counselor. Looking closely at those two seemingly simple words, we find depth not apparent at first glance. Wonderful represents marvelous, to excite wonder or admiration; to surprise; something strange; astonishing, exceeding natural power - Supernatural. Counselor means guide, director, instructor. The One who has all the answers, but must be sought for. We will receive answers from our Wonderful Counselor; however, we must seek those answers in His Word and through the Holy Spirit. We are promised if we do seek the truth, we will find it. Matthew 7:7 says,

"Ask, and it will be given to you; seek, and you will find; knock, and it will be opened to you."

Much of my impatience and frustrations are revealed through situations I do not really know how to handle; and yet, I want to be used by God to help others. The only way for me to be helpful in any situation is to fully rely on God, understand and share His counsel not mine. The only way to find His direction is to diligently study the Bible. I cannot control anything. I can only be available to allow God to use me for His work. I have to run to Him and seek refuge to be of any value. Refuge in God is interactive. God becomes our refuge by counseling us on how to walk in the way of life and not death, but we must seek His counsel in the Word. Psalm 119:24 adds, ***"Your testimonies are my delight; they are my counselors."***

This season, if you find yourself raising an independent teenager, helping a relative struggling in her marriage, reaching a friend tied up in addiction, or wanting wise counsel for a co-worker whose life seems to be coming apart, remember, you are not alone. You do not face the challenges alone. Seek counsel from Jesus our Wonderful Counselor who loves us! In 1 John 4:19, we are reminded, ***"We love because he first loved us."***

Courtroom of Life

Devotion #2 - Pastor Philip Piasecki

While I was in college, I held a lot of interesting jobs. I worked at a daycare for a couple of years, running around with the four and five-year-old kids. Then I got a job at a doctor's office as a Specimen Processor (running tests on blood), which I was not qualified to do. Lastly, I worked at the Oakland County Prosecutor's Office as a student worker. This job was incredibly interesting as I got to see the inner workings of the judicial system. One of my jobs was to put together case files of arrests from the night before. I saw some really interesting things, also some pretty brutal and sad things. The most nerve-racking part of the job was when we would have to run files over to the courthouse. I would have to walk into a courtroom while a trial was taking place, and give the file to the prosecutor that needed it. I would get to see the defendant's legal counsel giving them advice on what to answer, how to proceed, and what to say to the judge. Thinking back on these courtroom scenes, I cannot help but think about Jesus, our Wonderful Counselor.

The courtroom scene may be a bit dramatic, but we all find ourselves in situations where we are looking for counsel. The question is from where and to whom are we looking for this advice? I think of the story of Job, and how he looked to his friends for counsel, and they gave him terrible advice. I have seen many Christians slowly fall away from Christ because they continue to follow ungodly counsel in their lives. Jesus Christ, He is the Wonderful Counselor. He is the one that we need to be looking toward every day in our lives. I know that many times in the heat of the moment, we are faced with making decisions quickly. We may not have time to stop, pray about a decision, and then make that decision. This is why we need to be asking Christ for wisdom every day.

James 1:5 says, ***"If any of you lacks wisdom, let him ask God, who gives generously to all without reproach, and it will be given him."***

I think we can all acknowledge that we lack wisdom. Luckily for all of us, God gives wisdom generously to all who just ask! Our Wonderful Counselor will give us the wisdom that we need to make godly decisions in any situation that we may face. Think twice before you seek worldly counsel, and seek counsel from the Wonderful Counselor.

God's Job Description
Devotion #3 - Debbie Kerr

Can you recall the best Christmas gift you ever received? I mean, can you think of the one that made you squeal with delight? This time of year, we are inundated with television commercials for the latest and greatest products. The stores start announcing their doorbuster sales in early November. Black Friday now begins on Thanksgiving Day before your turkey has had a chance to digest. We can hardly wait to score the hottest ticket items for the best price! We stress and overschedule ourselves throughout December to make our holiday one to remember. If we are honest, we run ourselves ragged as if it is our job to make everyone on our list happy. When we put our hope in the commercialism of Christmas, we can almost guarantee disappointment and serious debt. If we can set aside the hustle and bustle of the season and focus on the true meaning of Christmas, it can be the most wonderful time of the year! However, it can also be one of the most difficult times of the year that can bring depression, heartache, loneliness, and pain.

Do you suppose it is a coincidence that the most difficult time of the year is also the same wonderful season we celebrate the greatest Gift of all, the birth of the Savior of the world? He is Immanuel, God with us! God in His abundant love and mercy sent His Only Son not just to save us from our sins but to also save us from ourselves! The prophet Isaiah foretold hundreds of years before Christ's birth the titles of Jesus, given to Him by the Father. One of the amazing titles and positions He possesses is our Wonderful Counselor. He is called Wonderful, or full of wonder! He is amazing, astonishing, awesome, and miraculous! If He is a miracle-working Counselor, then sign me up! He understands what our words cannot adequately articulate, counsels us in our decisions, and guides the best direction in life. In every season of life, He is there, ready to give us the counsel and wisdom that we need. He heals us from the inside out! Isaiah 61:1-3 gives us Jesus' job description as our Wonderful Counselor.

Isaiah 61:1-3 says, ***"The Spirit of the Lord God is upon me,***
  because the Lord has anointed me
to bring good news to the poor;
  he has sent me to bind up the brokenhearted,
to proclaim liberty to the captives,
  and the opening of the prison to those who are bound;
to proclaim the year of the Lord's favor,
  and the day of vengeance of our God;
  to comfort all who mourn;
to grant to those who mourn in Zion -
  to give them a beautiful headdress instead of ashes,
the oil of gladness instead of mourning,
  the garment of praise instead of a faint spirit;
that they may be called oaks of righteousness,
  the planting of the Lord, that he may be glorified."

God also uses earthly counselors as a very real source of comfort and help. There is no shame in counseling with a good Christian counselor, one who knows Jesus does the healing and will point us to His Word and His ways. Always remember that no one understands like Jesus.

Have you made your appointment with the Wonderful Counselor? Maybe a good God-counseling session is in order?

Know it All
Devotion #4 - Shawna Johnson

We all know a know-it-all. It is the person that has answers for everything and cannot be told otherwise; their way is always the best way. We listen to them, nod and shake our heads (as if we are listening), and walk away rolling our eyes. "Whatever dude," I think to myself, "You know it all." Then I sit back and think, "Yikes, sometimes I can be that person!"

Ask yourself, are you teachable? Coachable? Open to correction? Or are you that guy too? Does it have to be "my way or the highway?"

Proverbs 12:15 (NLT) says, **"Fools think their own way is right, but the wise listen to others."** Scripture just called us fools! That should be very humbling. Thankfully, the Lord is gracious and kind, and we do not have to remain this way. Praise Him! Let Him counsel us and lead us to wisdom.

Mediate on the following verses and give thanks that we do not have to know every answer. Rest knowing that the Lord will lead the way. Remember, after all, **"His name shall be called Wonderful Counselor"** (Isaiah 9:6).

Be teachable.

2 Timothy 3:16 says, **"All Scripture is breathed out by God and profitable for teaching, for reproof, for correction, and for training in righteousness, that the man of God may be complete, equipped for every good work."** God's Word is **"profitable for teaching"** if we are willing to be taught.

Be coachable.

Proverbs 19:20 says, *"Listen to advice and accept instruction, that you may gain wisdom in the future."* This verse seems a little redundant. To *"listen to advice"* sounds similar to *"accept instruction."* Maybe God is trying to get our attention.

Protect yourself.

Colossians 2:8 (NIV) says, *"See to it that no one takes you captive through hollow and deceptive philosophy, which depends on human tradition and the elemental spiritual forces of this world rather than on Christ."* Be careful not to be prideful due to an overestimation of one's own knowledge. Guard your mind and heart.

Praise Him.

Psalm 16:7-8 (NIV) says, *"I will praise the Lord, who counsels me; even at night my heart instructs me. I keep my eyes always on the Lord. With him at my right hand, I will not be shaken."* Receive wisdom from God, use it, and thank Him. Praise is an expression of thankfulness.

Listen.

James 1:19 says, *"Know this, my beloved brothers: let every person be quick to hear, slow to speak, slow to anger."* Keep your mouth shut. You might learn something from someone else!

Rest.

Psalm 73:24 (NIV) says, *"You guide me with your counsel, and afterward you will take me into glory."* The reward of accepting the counsel of the Lord is rest.

Wonderful Christmastime
Devotion #5 - Pastor Noble Baird

Christmas is always an exciting time of year. Being in Michigan, we are blessed with all four seasons, two of which are usually filled with snow! For those of you who know me, I love music. One of the greatest privileges I have ever received is being able to worship on the worship team at church together with my wife, Haley. Growing up, my father and I have always listened to The Beatles. Sadly, my wife does not share the same love for them as my father and I do, but there is still time! In 1979, Paul McCartney wrote a song titled, *"Wonderful Christmastime."* It is a song about coming together during Christmas and simply enjoying the wonderful season together.

By definition, wonderful means "to be excited." In Matthew 1:20-25, we have the account of Joseph's interaction with an angel of the Lord. Matthew writes, **"But as he considered these things, behold, an angel of the Lord appeared to him in a dream, saying, 'Joseph, son of David, do not fear to take Mary as your wife, for that which is conceived in her is from the Holy Spirit. She will bear a son, and you shall call his name Jesus, for he will save his people from their sins.' All this took place to fulfill what the Lord had spoken by the prophet: 'Behold, the virgin shall conceive and bear a son, and they shall call his name Immanuel' (which means, God with us). When Joseph woke from sleep, he did as the angel of the Lord commanded him: he took his wife but knew her not until she had given birth to a son. And he called his name Jesus."** There is no doubt that this time in Joseph's life was scary, frightful, painful, and then exciting and truly wonderful all at the same time! He finds his fiancé, Mary, pregnant. Then, he decides to end the engagement quietly; however, that is when God steps in, and he is given the wonderful news about Jesus.

The name *"Wonderful Counselor"* is only recorded once. It is in Isaiah 9:6. When we look at this account of the Christmas season, there is no doubt that it is truly a wonderful time! Joseph's heartbreak was turned into exciting news about the truly wonderful Savior that was prophesied about for centuries! As we continue in this Christmas season (maybe you will even hear *"Wonderful Christmastime"* on the radio), I challenge you to take a step back and remember the truly wonderful season it is. Also, remember the Wonderful Counselor whose birth we celebrate during this time.

Letters to My Little Ones

Devotion #6 - Pastor Ryan Story

A letter to my children:

There will never be a point in your life when I will not be here to give you godly advice. As long as I have breath in my lungs, I will not cease to help you in life. I want to see you be victorious over anything the enemy throws at you. I want you to run towards God with such a purpose, you shed any weight that is slowing you down. I want to see you prosper in whatever Jesus has planned for you. I get overly excited even thinking about how amazing you are and are going to be.

I have lived a life of making too many unwise choices that I will do anything to make sure you do not go through the same pain as I have. I have sat back and watched myself and many people who I have deeply loved to make choices that are void of any wisdom. Ironically, James 1:5 says, **"If any of you lacks wisdom, let him ask God, who gives generously to all without reproach, and it will be given him."** My hope for your life is that you learn how to keep wisdom as the cornerstone of your walk with God. I have lived a life where I did not try to seek out becoming wise until I was older. I do not wish that upon any of you. Learn to plead with God for wisdom because He will give it to you. Make sure you use that wisdom to help others because that is what God will want to see. Gifts are only good when you share them.

Grow up in such a way that you realize how much more you will be able to do for God if you seek out wisdom. There will be a point in your life when someone is going to come to you and need advice. I pray you are able to take a page out of Jesus' Book and be able to counsel them. We live in such a world that needs more people to have godly wisdom. The church has many smart followers, but few wise leaders, and I want you to be wise beyond your years.

In Isaiah, one of the names used to foretell about His coming is **"Wonderful Counselor."** I pray that you run, plead, and are relentless in your pursuit of wisdom. Instead of asking God, "Why is this happening," learn to ask, "Why is this best for my life?" Instead of being caught off guard by any rough times, be wise enough to know He is in control. Know that at any moment in your life, you can turn to a God that has your tomorrow already worked out. Never be too proud to ask for help.

Never be too lazy to pray.

Never be too busy to help those God puts in your life.

Mighty God

Dr. Randy T. Johnson

My niece and her husband have triplets, identical twin boys and a girl. I remember when they were four and full of energy. When you tease with one, you get all three. I asked Erika if my hair was curlier than hers. She exclaimed, "You do not have any hair!" I acted astonished as I grabbed my bald scalp. I then pretended to cut her hair and both boys with my fingers. She boldly announced that she had a superpower. Her amazing power was to grow her hair back quickly.

1. What superpower would you like to have?
_____
_____
_____

Superheroes have been introduced with all kinds of powers: Teleportation, invisibility, flight, x-ray vision, time travel, and superhuman strength. Isaiah 9:6 introduces us to the greatest "superhero" of all time, **"For to us a child is born, to us a son is given; and the government shall be upon his shoulder, and his name shall be called Wonderful Counselor, Mighty God, Everlasting Father, Prince of Peace."**

He is the **"Mighty God."** It can be translated as "God is mighty" or "God is a mighty warrior."

The Mighty God is a warrior.

This child (Jesus) is called a Mighty God. He was and is a warrior. He is not a wimp. Psalm 24:8 says, **"Who is this King of glory? The Lord, strong and mighty, the Lord, mighty in battle!"** David repeats himself to make sure his point is clear. He uses a question to emphasize his point. The Lord is mighty. He is a battle-tested warrior.

Psalm 147:5 adds, **"Great is our Lord, and abundant in power; his understanding is beyond measure."** Power and understanding are a great combination. He knows what to do and has the power to back it up.

2. What are some examples that show Jesus as a warrior?
___
___
___

Isaiah 64:8 points out that the Lord created us, *"But now, O Lord, you are our Father; we are the clay, and you are our potter; we are all the work of your hand."* Scripture repeatedly points out that God created us. He created something from nothing.

Isaiah 40:28 adds, *"Have you not known? Have you not heard? The Lord is the everlasting God, the Creator of the ends of the earth. He does not faint or grow weary; his understanding is unsearchable."* Again, we have questions used to get our attention. The Lord is powerful and does not wear down. He just keeps going, and going, and going.

3. How is this passage comforting and challenging to us?
___
___
___

Zephaniah 3:17 says, *"The Lord your God is in your midst, a mighty one who will save; he will rejoice over you with gladness; he will quiet you by his love; he will exult over you with loud singing."*

4. How does the Lord use His mighty power?
___
___
___

5. Do you believe we are called to be warriors? If so, how?

_____
_____
_____

John Piper wrote, "Jesus is the Lion of Judah (Revelation 5:5) and the Lamb of God (Revelation 5:6) - He was lionhearted and lamblike, strong and meek, tough and tender, aggressive and responsive, bold and brokenhearted. He sets the pattern for manhood."

The Mighty God cannot be manhandled.

The Lord does not misuse His power. He cannot be manipulated, tricked, or bribed. Deuteronomy 10:17 says, *"For the Lord your God is God of gods and Lord of lords, the great, the mighty, and the awesome God, who is not partial and takes no bribe."* Moses says, "My Dad is bigger than your dad." The Lord is the greatest God and loftiest Lord. He is mighty and even awesome. Moses adds a side note: The Lord is fair and honest.

6. How is this verse comforting and challenging?

_____
_____
_____

7. What comes to mind when you see or hear the word "awesome"?

_____
_____
_____

Paul reiterates the concept of the Lord being fair and honest in Romans 1:4, *"And was declared to be the Son of God in power according to the Spirit of holiness by his resurrection from the dead, Jesus Christ our Lord."*

8. What can happen when *"power"* and *"holiness"* do not go together?

_____
_____
_____

Martin Luther knew he could trust the Lord. He wrote, "I have held many things in my hands, and have lost them all; but whatever I have placed in God's hands, that I still possess."

9. Why do we place things in God's hands? How?

_____
_____
_____

The Mighty God has the power to accomplish His purposes.

The Lord has a plan for our lives. He wants us to follow Him in salvation and repentance. Holiness and obedience are important to Him. Paul states that Jesus' title also describes His mission. Titus 2:13 says, *"Waiting for our blessed hope, the appearing of the glory of our great God and Savior Jesus Christ."*

10. What comes to mind when you see the title *"Savior"*?

_____
_____
_____

David asks a great question in Psalm 8:3-4, *"When I look at your heavens, the work of your fingers, the moon and the stars, which you have set in place, what is man that you are mindful of him, and the son of man that you care for him?"* David points out that God created everything, but that He gives special attention to people.

11. What does the word *"mindful"* mean and imply?

_____

_____

_____

Finally, Jeremiah 29:11 points out that God has a plan for our lives, *"For I know the plans I have for you, declares the Lord, plans for welfare and not for evil, to give you a future and a hope."*

12. How does the Lord's title of "Mighty God" relate to Him having a plan for our lives?

_____

_____

_____

Finally, think about Franklin Graham's statement, "There is no question that America has been a nation that has been blessed by almighty God. There is no other nation in the history of mankind that has done what His nation has done - and it's because of God's hand and His blessing."

Notes

Having Complete Power
Devotion #1 - Pastor Philip Piasecki

There is nothing worse than feeling powerless. As humans, we always want to have some control over our lives. I remember driving my brother and myself to school one dark January morning when we hit a patch of ice on the freeway exit ramp. Instantly, I went from having complete control of my car, to having none at all. We spun 180 degrees to where we could see a semi-truck heading straight for us. By the grace of God, I had the awareness to pull the wheel and slide us off into the ditch. My brother and I sat there speechless. I finally looked over at him and said: "Don't tell mom about this." Years later, we finally told my parents the story, and about how differently that morning could have gone for the both of us. Sometimes in life, we can have this same feeling; it seems like our whole life is out of control, and that we have no power over what is happening. This is when we need to fix our eyes on the One who is the Mighty God.

The word almighty means "having complete power." I am sure that is not the first thought that came to everyone's mind when Jesus was first born as a baby. It is hard to imagine a tiny baby, that needs milk and needs to be changed, as having complete power. However, Jesus was fully God as well as fully man. God is almighty. Therefore, Jesus is almighty. When Jesus was born, He may not have been what the Jewish people were expecting for their king, but Jesus knew how His plan of redemption was going to unfold. Do we trust in Jesus as our Almighty God? I know that in my life, many times I put Christ in a box. I put limitations on what He can do, sometimes without even knowing it. However, it is evident in my prayers, my thoughts, and my actions. I know that if I daily approached Jesus as my Almighty God, I would see drastic changes in my life.

We see an incredible picture of who Jesus is in Psalm 24:8-10, **"Who is this King of glory? The Lord, strong and mighty, the**

Lord, mighty in battle! Lift up your heads, O gates! And lift them up, O ancient doors, that the King of glory may come in. Who is this King of glory? The Lord of hosts, he is the King of glory!"

Our Lord is strong and mighty. He is mighty in battle. He is fighting for us every day. There is no reason to hang our heads; we need to lift them up to the One who is mighty to save us. Life does not always bring what we are expecting, but Jesus is there for us no matter what comes our way. He is the Mighty God, who holds complete power. Expect that He will show up in mighty ways in your own life.

Letters to My Little Ones
Devotion #2 - Pastor Ryan Story

A letter to my children:

The things that God is going to do with your lives are unfathomable! I cannot even begin to figure out what you will be. Will you be calm or wild? Will you have a thirst for righteousness and a heart for those in need? Will you be logical and loving? I cannot even begin to think what your personality will be like, to even think about what God is going to do with your life. Even though I do not know much about you, knowing you will be used by God is such a fantastic feeling. The biggest dreams I can dream for you are still infinitesimal compared to what God has planned for you! God can do so many things with one small child. When Jesus was born, angels rejoiced so much they became visible. A group of shepherds' lives were changed at the sight of a small baby. A temple priest by the name of Simeon said he saw salvation when he held that small baby. Wise men traveled miles to meet a small boy that lived under a star. Jesus was mighty from the moment He was born. God can do mighty things with small babies. While you may not be able to boast of that kind of might, know that God loves using small things.

The prophet Zechariah said, **"For who dares make light of small beginnings"** (Zechariah 4:10, NET). I cannot think of anything smaller than a baby, and I cannot think of anything larger than your potential. The largest tree starts as a small seed, but with the proper nurturing look at how tall it can grow. Some of the biggest companies that exist started in a garage or a basement. At one point, I did not know anything about the Bible. At one point, I did not know anything about Jesus. Years have passed and with a lot of hard work and being faithful to God; I am now trusted to teach the Bible to God's people. I know God will be there to help you move whatever mountains are in your life, just never lose faith that He, in fact, can and will move them. Do not look at your limitations; look at God's limitless power!

You all started out small, and have moved mountains in my heart. I cannot even begin to express how much I love you. I can only imagine how you will be able to be used by God to influence others and me. Never forget, size is not the same as power. Remember God used David to defeat Goliath. God only has one option: He must use the small to show His might. So let God show His might through you.

El Gibbor
Devotion #3 - Donna Fox

It seems everyone is searching for something (or someone) to fill a void in their life. Until we find Jesus, we are empty. This was me as a child and young adult. My father was an alcoholic. Life was not pleasant a lot of the time. I would lie in bed at night, listening to the fighting and commotion, thinking that there has got to be something out there I am missing in my life. I longed for peace. God offers peace, **"And the peace of God, which surpasses all understanding, will guard your hearts and your minds in Christ Jesus"** (Philippians 4:7).

I used to watch *"Superman"* on TV. Lois Lane would get herself into a predicament, and mild-mannered Clark Kent would transform into her superhero and rescue her. One time she was falling off the roof of a building several stories high, and of course, at the last moment, Superman swooped down and caught her. I was searching for that hero, someone to rescue me.

I needed a warrior, a strong, powerful Savior to enter my life and rescue me. My father did not fill that role. My brothers did not either. Not even my husband, as wonderful as he was (and is) could fit the role. He was not that "superhero" I needed to rescue me. I wanted a mighty warrior. In Hebrew, Mighty God is translated as "El Gibbor," the ultimate power over all. I longed for an "El Gibbor" in my life. I finally found him on April 24, 1995!

When I was introduced to Jesus and began a relationship with Him, I was rescued! A Mighty God had come into my life, and I knew He would fill the void. This was what I was searching for all my life. I was finally fulfilled and at peace. This was the superhero I needed in my life. One that would always be there to protect me, comfort me, and love me. In Hebrews 13:5, He said, **"I will never leave you nor forsake you."**

I spent years expecting someone to "save" me, a Savior. The Jews did as well. As prophesied in Isaiah and throughout the Old Testament, the Jews were expecting the Messiah to come and rescue them. When He did come, some recognized Jesus as the expected One; some did not. When your Savior calls out for you, do you recognize it is the Mighty God?

You are falling off the rooftop. You are almost to the first floor and then the ground. A Mighty God is reaching out to catch you and rescue you from certain death. Will you accept Him into your life? He is just waiting for you to believe and start a relationship with Him; then the void in your life will be filled with His peace and love!

My Hero

Devotion #4 - Angela Cox

"For to us a child is born, to us a son is given; and the government shall be upon his shoulder, and his name shall be called Wonderful Counselor, Mighty God, Everlasting Father, Prince of Peace." Isaiah 9:6

What does it mean to you when you hear, **"Mighty God"**? You think of something powerful, strong, and maybe even large or astounding. In Hebrew, the phrase **"Mighty God"** translates to "El Gibbor" which can mean a God-Like Hero. He is our Hero! He is our healer and our strength! Wow; what a **"Mighty God"** we serve.

Deuteronomy 10:17 says, **"For the Lord your God is God of gods and Lord of lords, the great, the mighty, and the awesome God, who is not partial and takes no bribe."** This divine title can only describe God. We can simply read the text and know that the plans of Jesus were put in place so that He would be King. However, how often has Jesus been just that in your life? Who knew that the names written on His life before His arrival would truly mean so much?

I walked through one of the hardest seasons of my life just a few years ago. Not knowing what the outcome would be for my life or my children, I pushed through and leaned on Jesus. God came through in mighty ways as I learned to grow in Him and be refined by His Word. I was and am in awe of Him and just how mighty He is, but through it all He was loving. Our **"Mighty God"** is strong but remember that this means He is gentle and loving as well. Our **"Mighty God"** came to this world as a baby to love us all and bring us freedom in His name.

How Mighty is Your God?

Devotion #5 - Kenny Hovis

How many times have you had an instance to question whether God can help you overcome a circumstance in your life? We have so many opportunities to wonder if He is paying attention. Does He see us suffering? Does He care about a family member or our illness? Does He understand our loss of a job? Does He feel the passing of a loved one? Does He see how little money is in our bank account? Does He sense our loneliness? Does He know our feeling that no one cares for us? I have been in the desert of self-pity that accentuates so many of these feelings. You get to a place where you feel abandoned, a true sense of hopelessness. No matter your best efforts, you feel God does not care.

A few years back I was self-employed. We always seemed to be struggling to make ends meet. We could not afford health insurance and started praying for God to show us what we needed to do. How can we grow the business? Should I work harder, more hours? Should we sell our house? A couple of years went by, and I was offered a position with Oxford Township Parks and Recreation. It was a modest salary but had phenomenal insurance and benefits. I thought I would retire from there. God answered our prayers.

All the while working there, I had plenty of vacation time, and it allowed me the opportunity to go on many prison trips with the HIM Prison Ministry. I found that most of the men I talked to in prison felt these same feelings of despair, abandonment, loneliness, and doubt. I have concluded when faced with life's challenges, many of us have these feelings.

I was reading from the Psalms and came upon this passage: **"For God alone, O my soul, wait in silence, for my hope is from him. He only is my rock and my salvation, my fortress; I shall not be** *shaken. On God rests my salvation and my glory; my mighty rock, my refuge is God"* (Psalm 62:5-7).

As I read this passage, it just jumped out at me. Duh! We are not meant to try and solve our problems on our own. We are to put our cares and despairs in His hands. We cannot fix our lives and problems ourselves. We are supposed to surround ourselves in the safe confines of the fortress that God is. Only there will we not be shaken. He is the originator of our hope.

I have come to a place in my faith where I believe it is all about focus. We focus on all that we may not have instead of turning 180 degrees and focusing on the fact God provides for us. He loves us. He protects us.

My God is mighty enough to take care of any situation, care, or concern. How mighty is your God?

Mighty to Save

Devotion #6 - Pastor Noble Baird

Back when I was just beginning to learn drums, one of the first worship songs I learned to play was, *"Mighty to Save"* by Hillsong United. I still remember my best friend, Pete, playing the opening guitar riff as he counted me in on the drums to begin what ended up being the first beat I learned. We were just a couple of teenagers playing in the youth worship band, but it was some of the most amazing worship experiences I have ever had the privilege of being a part. Within the chorus of this song, Hillsong wrote:

> Saviour, He can move the mountains
> My God is mighty to save
> He is mighty to save
> Forever Author of Salvation
> He rose and conquered the grave
> Jesus conquered the grave.

In this study, we have been going over the different names of Christ during this Christmas season. This week is one of my favorites, Mighty God. Although we only see the actual name "Mighty God" in Isaiah 9:6, we continually see our God's might all throughout His Word. In 1 Peter 1:3-5, Peter writes about the words which we echo in the chorus of *"Mighty to Save,"* **"Blessed be the God and Father of our Lord Jesus Christ! According to his great mercy, he has caused us to be born again to a living hope through the resurrection of Jesus Christ from the dead, to an inheritance that is imperishable, undefiled, and unfading, kept in heaven for you, who by God's power are being guarded through faith for a salvation ready to be revealed in the last time."** Here, Peter reminds us of the hope we have in Christ through His death and resurrection.

I love this song because it perfectly depicts the Mighty God we have. During this Christmas season, it is not always easy. I know that there are those of you who dread and even hate this time of year, because of the pain and hurt that you are experiencing. However, I want to encourage you to remember the words of this chorus. Remember the Mighty God that we serve and have, never forgetting that He truly can move those mountains in our life and that no matter what, He has already conquered the grave for you and me. Yeah, we truly have a Mighty God and a mighty Savior!

Everlasting Father

Dr. Randy T. Johnson

I remember hearing a riddle about a father and son who were in a bad car accident. The father was killed. The son was rushed to the hospital. He needs surgery. As soon as the surgeon gets ready to make the first cut, the surgeon says, "I cannot operate – that boy is my son."

1. How is this scenario possible?
   _____
   _____
   _____

Isaiah 9:6 brings an interesting scenario, *"For to us a child is born, to us a son is given; and the government shall be upon his shoulder, and his name shall be called Wonderful Counselor, Mighty God, Everlasting Father, Prince of Peace."* A child is called the *"Everlasting Father."* Normally, a newborn child is not referred to as a father.

2. How is the Messiah the *"Everlasting Father"* while being a child?
   _____
   _____
   _____

3. Do any of the titles in this verse imply the deity of Jesus?
   _____
   _____
   _____

John Martin gives an interesting summary in the *"Bible Knowledge Commentary:"*

"This Deliverer will also be called the Everlasting Father. Many people are puzzled by this title because the Messiah, God's Son, is distinguished in the Trinity from God the Father. How can the Son be the Father? Several things must be noted in this regard. First, the Messiah, being the second Person of the Trinity, is in His essence,

God. Therefore He has all the attributes of God including eternality. Since God is One (even though He exists in three Persons), the Messiah is God. Second, the title 'Everlasting Father' is an idiom used to describe the Messiah's relationship to time, not His relationship to the other Members of the Trinity. He is said to be everlasting, just as God (the Father) is called 'the Ancient of Days' (Daniel 7:9). The Messiah will be a 'fatherly' Ruler. Third, perhaps Isaiah had in mind the promise to David (2 Samuel 7:16) about the 'foreverness' of the kingdom which God promised would come through David's line. The Messiah, a Descendant of David, will fulfill this promise for which the nation had been waiting."

Isaiah 63:16 adds, **"For you are our Father, though Abraham does not know us, and Israel does not acknowledge us; you, O Lord, are our Father, our Redeemer from of old is your name."**

4. How does this relate to the **"Everlasting Father"** title?
_____
_____
_____

Everlasting Father refers to Jesus' deity.

Jesus is God, and He knows it. In John 10:30, He says, **"I and the Father are one."**

5. What did Jesus mean by this verse?
_____
_____
_____

He adds in John 14:9, **"Jesus said to him, 'Have I been with you so long, and you still do not know me, Philip? Whoever has seen me has seen the Father. How can you say, 'Show us the Father?'"**

6. What did Jesus mean by this verse?

_____
_____
_____

Everlasting Father refers to Jesus' love.

Oswald Chambers pointed out, "In the midst of the awesomeness, a touch comes, and you know it is the right hand of Jesus Christ. You know it is not the hand of restraint, correction, nor chastisement, but the right hand of the Everlasting Father. Whenever His hand is laid upon you, it gives inexpressible peace and comfort, and the sense that 'underneath are the everlasting arms,' (Deuteronomy 33:27) full of support, provision, comfort and strength."

As we have seen from John 14:9, Jesus equates Himself with the Father. Psalm 68:5 speaks of the love of the Father, *"Father of the fatherless and protector of widows is God in his holy habitation."*

1 Corinthians 8:6 says, *"Yet for us there is one God, the Father, from whom are all things and for whom we exist, and one Lord, Jesus Christ, through whom are all things and through whom we exist."* Ephesians 4:6 adds, *"One God and Father of all, who is over all and through all and in all."* God is clearly referred to as the Father.

7. What positive connotations come to mind when you think of a father?

_____
_____
_____

8. What should a father look like?

_____
_____
_____

9. How is Jesus a loving Father?

_____
_____
_____

Romans 8:15-16 says, **"For you did not receive the spirit of slavery to fall back into fear, but you have received the Spirit of adoption as sons, by whom we cry, 'Abba! Father!' The Spirit himself bears witness with our spirit that we are children of God."**

10. How can we become children of God?

_____
_____
_____

Revelation 1:8 says, **"'I am the Alpha and the Omega,' says the Lord God, 'who is and who was and who is to come, the Almighty.'"** Jesus is God. He always has been, is, and always will be. He is the Everlasting Father.

In the 1500's Francis de Sales said, "The same everlasting Father who cares for you today will care for you tomorrow and every day. Either he will shield you from suffering or give you unfailing strength to bear it. Be at peace then and put aside all anxious thoughts and imaginings."

11. How does Jesus' title of Everlasting Father comfort, encourage, challenge, and motivate you?

_____
_____
_____

Charles Spurgeon spoke these words, "How complex is the person of our Lord Jesus Christ! Almost in the same breath, the prophet calls him a 'child,' and a 'counselor,' a 'son,' and 'the everlasting Father.' This is no contradiction, and to us scarcely a paradox, but it is a mighty marvel that he who was an infant should at the same time be infinite, he who was the Man of Sorrows should also be God over all, blessed for ever; and that he who is in the Divine Trinity always called the Son, should nevertheless be correctly called 'the everlasting Father.'"

Notes

Gobstopper

Devotion #1 - Michael Fox

"For to us a child is born, to us a son is given; and the government shall be upon his shoulder, and his name shall be called Wonderful Counselor, Mighty God, Everlasting Father, Prince of Peace." Isaiah 9:6

When I thought of the phrase **"Everlasting Father,"** two things came to mind. They were my dad and an Everlasting Gobstopper. I am honestly not sure where the Gobstopper came from. I do not eat them often, and I can also assure you that they are not everlasting. However, it appears the makers of the Gobstopper want you to believe that. Still, in this weird moment, it helped me frame what may be everlasting means.

First, I want to address the topic of my dad. My biological father is undoubtedly the closest thing on Earth comparable to God our Father. My dad raised me; my dad taught me. My dad has been there "forever," and while he is still with me on this Earth, I can see how his legacy will live on in my life even after he may move on to Heaven. I regularly remember things he has told me over the years and still, as an adult, I am applying these things to my life now. I am sure this will remain true for the rest of my life. This naturally leads to the concept of forever.

In Psalm 72:17, God's name is spoken of as forever: **"May his name endure forever, his fame continue as long as the sun! May people be blessed in him, all nations call him blessed!"** His name will endure forever!

In Revelation 21:6-7, we are called His son: **"And he said to me, 'It is done! I am the Alpha and the Omega, the beginning and the end. To the thirsty I will give from the spring of the water *of life without payment. The one who conquers will have this heritage, and I will be his God and he will be my son.'* The Lord references His followers as His children.

John 3:16 is likely not new for many: *"For God so loved the world, that he gave his only Son, that whoever believes in him should not perish but have eternal life."* God has invited us to be His son. He will be our *"Everlasting Father."* All we need to do is believe in Him and confess Him as our Lord. I look forward to spending eternity in Heaven with my *"Everlasting Father."* If you cannot call Him your *"Everlasting Father"* yet, I encourage you to know it is that simple, and we would love to help you know Him. For those of you who can call Him your *"Everlasting Father,"* it is a great reminder that we have that our Father is looking out for us every day for the rest of eternity.

Never Leave Nor Forsake
Devotion #2 - Pastor Philip Piasecki

Being a father has drastically changed my approach to life. After my daughter was born, my main priority became being the best father I could be. Every action and decision that I made started being run through the filter of being a father. I have always been a huge thrill seeker; however, I am now much less likely to do something that could put my life in danger now that I am a dad. I always want to be there for my kids, and it breaks my heart to see those whose fathers have abandoned them. The lack of good fathers is truly an epidemic in our culture today. There are so many kids that just want to know they have a dad who loves them, and they have been deprived of that opportunity so far in their life. However, Christmas can be an incredible reminder of the Everlasting Father that we have through the person of Jesus Christ.

When Scripture calls Jesus **"Everlasting Father,"** do not be confused, it is not mistaking Him for God the Father. However, Jesus is the perfect representation of God the Father's attributes. Through Jesus, we see fatherly love. In Scripture, we see Jesus love His friends, His disciples, and strangers, and ultimately lay His life down for all of those people. A father never abandons his children. Still to this day, if I need help with something, I know that I can call my dad and he will be there right away. In Hebrews, we see the fatherly character of Christ.

Hebrews 13:5-6 says, **"Keep your life free from love of money, and be content with what you have, for he has said, 'I will never leave you nor forsake you.' So we can confidently say, 'The Lord is my helper; I will not fear; what can man do to me?'"**

This Scripture serves as an important reminder that true contentment comes from knowing that the Lord is with us, and will never leave us. It does not matter what worldly possessions we have or how life is treating us, we can celebrate knowing that the Lord is with us. Jesus Christ, the Everlasting Father, will never leave us or forsake us. He does not bail when life gets rough, and He does not give up on us when we fail Him. He cares for us, He watches over us, He encourages us, He disciplines us, and He treats us like a father treats his children. If you do not have a loving earthly father, know that God is your Heavenly Father whose perfect attributes were put on display for the world to see through His son Jesus Christ. If you are a dad reading this, I challenge you to have your actions towards your children reflect those of our perfect Heavenly Father. Even when it may feel like we are alone, take hope in knowing that God and Jesus Christ are always there for us.

Willy Wonka

Devotion #3 - Jeremy Smith

"For to us a child is born, to us a son is given; and the government shall be upon his shoulder, and his name shall be called Wonderful Counselor, Mighty God, Everlasting Father, Prince of Peace." Isaiah 9:6

The emphasis this week has been focusing on the **"Everlasting Father."** As I read and began to collect my thoughts, I was reminded of Willy Wonka and the Chocolate Factory. I know it is a bit strange, but as they are traveling through the chocolate factory they make a stop at a machine that is all covered. Wonka is asked about the machine and he begins to explain the idea he had. The idea was to have a candy that someone could get one time and not need to worry that it would only temporarily satisfy them. He agrees to give them each an Everlasting Gobstopper. Everlasting is very simply defined as never-ending. Candy cannot be everlasting. Actually, it often creates a desire for more.

When I think of a father or the role of a father, I begin to think of what is my own expectation and what roles I need to fulfill with my own children. When I have something I have never done before or need help on a project, one of my first calls is to my dad. Proverbs 22:6 tells us, *"Train up a child in the way he should go; even when he is old he will not depart from it."* It seems like an almost weekly occurrence now, but one of my kids asks why I have to go to work. In 1 Timothy 5:8, we are given the biblical explanation of being a provider, *"But if anyone does not provide for his relatives, and especially for members of his household, he has denied the faith and is worse than an unbeliever."* Of course, there is still a balance, and needs to be disciplined from time to time. Proverbs 13:24 adds, *"Whoever spares the rod hates his son, but he who loves him is diligent to discipline him."* Also, there still needs to be a relationship there. The relationship can only develop and blossom when we work on it. Deuteronomy 6:6-9 tells us what God's expectation is, **"And these words that I command you today shall be on your heart. You shall teach them diligently to your children, and shall talk of them when you sit in your house, and when you walk by the way, and when you lie down, and when you rise. You shall bind them as a sign on your hand, and they shall be as frontlets between your eyes. You shall write them on the doorposts of your house and on your gates."** These are some of the many verses we find throughout the Bible that give us a biblical direction of the roles and expectations of being a father. God is willing to be our **"Everlasting Father"** and regularly does all these things with and for us.

To easily and definitively explain an **"Everlasting Father,"** we can take a look at any of the individual roles the Bible has clearly outlined, and realize that it is a never-ending example or expectation of what it will be like to follow God. It does not matter where we come from or what experiences we have had with our own earthly father. All we need to do is believe that Jesus came to Earth and died for our sins, was buried but rose again, and we have accepted the invitation to be adopted into His family. That gives us an **"Everlasting Father."**

The Child is the Everlasting Father

Devotion #4 - Pastor Kyle Wendel

"For to us a child is born, to us a son is given; and the government shall be upon his shoulder, and his name shall be called Wonderful Counselor, Mighty God, Everlasting Father, Prince of Peace." Isaiah 9:6

It is incredible to look at this verse and see some of the characteristics of Jesus revealed in this prophecy. **"Wonderful Counselor," "Mighty God," "Everlasting Father,"** and **"Prince of Peace"** are titles with so much meaning attached to them. I love how the Bible shows us so much of who God is and how much of a mystery He can still be simply because He is God and above our understanding. The beauty of it is that God still reveals who He is to us.

The characteristic of Jesus being an **"Everlasting Father"** is an incredible thing to see and realize. To know that Jesus is everlasting, eternal, and forever is a powerful truth. Jesus is not just a man that was in history. Jesus not only lived and died. Jesus is forever. His Kingdom is forever. His power is forever. There is no end to Jesus. There is no end to His greatness. His fatherhood will have no end.

Colossians 1:16 says, *"For by him all things were created, in heaven and on earth, visible and invisible, whether thrones or dominions or rulers or authorities - all things were created through him and for him."*

This verse in Colossians helps us see that all things were created by and through Jesus. Some will try to say that Jesus was just another creation of God. That is not true when you look through the Bible. Jesus is God. Jesus is Creator. Jesus is the **"Everlasting Father."** All things are created through Him and for Him.

John 15:13 adds, **"Greater love has no one than this, that someone lay down his life for his friends."**

One of the ultimate roles of a father is to protect and provide for their children. The Child to be born was the **"Everlasting Father."** He was to protect and provide for His people. We see that Jesus would ultimately go to the cross to save His people; to give a way for all people to be saved. It was to show the true act of protection and provision. He provided Himself out of love as the sacrifice to be slain. By what Jesus did alone on the cross, we now have the opportunity to be saved from the punishment of our sin. This is the love of God. This is the **"Everlasting Father"** who conquered sin and death for His children. How incredible it is to see this truth. We have a Father who would do anything for His children. There is nothing that can stop Jesus. His Kingdom and reign will be everlasting.

Let us worship our **"Wonderful Counselor," "Mighty God," "Everlasting Father,"** and **"Prince of Peace"** with everything that we are. He deserves all the glory and worship.

How does seeing Jesus as an **"Everlasting Father"** change your perspective about Him?

Letters to My Little Ones
Devotion #5 - Pastor Ryan Story

A letter to my children:

I cannot be there for you every step of the way. I wish I could be there to watch every moment of your life, but I might have to miss a few important events in your life. I may have to walk out of the room, and you will fall off of something. I may not be around when your siblings gang up on you and hurt you. It is humbling to know that I cannot be the type of father that can be everywhere at once. My extent as a father has limits. As much as I would love to be Superman, I know my shortcomings. I will never stop trying to live up to the Superman legacy, but I want you to always count on one person more than me, and no it is not your mother.

I want to be there for you no matter what. There is never anything you can do that would make me not love you. I am a wreck of a person; I will at times fail you. God, however, will never fail you. He always has to be perfect. As much as I will attempt to be there for you in your life, He will be there more. David writes in Psalm 103:13, **"As a father shows compassion to his children, so the LORD shows compassion to those who fear Him."** In my life, I pray to show you compassion for others. I know I am falling far short of this. My emotional responses to compassion seemed to have malfunctioned years ago. I promise I will get better. I do not want you to grow up thinking God is cold like your father. I want you to grow up to know God as compassionate, loving, kind, and caring. Children must look to their fathers to show them compassion.

Now I am going to have to address a tough theological issue with you, my children. If I can teach you anything, it will be "know your Trinity." It is weird to read about the fore coming of the Messiah, the Son of God, Jesus, and hear that His name is described as

"Everlasting Father." Breaking your brain over the ins and outs of doctrine, know that because of Jesus, God's fatherly character to us is revealed. If there is ever a moment you want to know what God is like as a father, look to the perfect image of God, Jesus. I pray I can emulate this to the point people see your Everlasting Father in your actions because you see His actions in your earthly father.

Compassion

Devotion #6 - Pastor John Carter

Isaiah 9:6 says, *"For to us a child is born, to us a son is given; and the government shall be upon his shoulder, and his name shall be called Wonderful Counselor, Mighty God, Everlasting Father, Prince of Peace."*

In our current culture and country, the role of the father has been diminished quite significantly; our view of what a father is may seem obscure to many. Watching T.V. will quickly show you that the modern father is portrayed as a weak role, a position that is not respected or revered. Often the character is played like one that is ignorant, incompetent, or downright wicked. I assume this role is played out because that is what the majority of people have experienced in their own life. As we see Jesus described here in Isaiah, He is given the title *"Everlasting Father,"* we must be careful not to associate our perceptions of what a father is onto Jesus.

Jesus is described as *"Everlasting Father"* meaning that He has always been and will always be the founder of our faith. It is easy to forget that everlasting part of the title. That means forever, always, and in all situations. He is our father when things are difficult, when things are going well, when we make mistakes, and when we do not make mistakes. It is forever! We must be careful not to respond to Jesus as our Father in the same way that we respond to our earthly fathers. We may find ourselves putting guilt and shame where guilt and shame have already been handled. When we humble ourselves, repent, and put our trust in Jesus, we give Him the shame and guilt that comes with sin. How awesome is it to have a Savior that has an intimate understanding of what a good father should be? Psalm 103:13 (NASB) says, *"Just as a father has compassion on his children, So the LORD has compassion on those who fear Him."*

I hope today, you will reflect on how good our Heavenly Father is. He is kind, just, and merciful. Maybe you can relate to this with your earthly father, maybe not. Either way, we have an example to look to in Jesus as our Eternal Father.

Prince of Peace

Dr. Randy T. Johnson

"For to us a child is born, to us a son is given; and the government shall be upon his shoulder, and his name shall be called Wonderful Counselor, Mighty God, Everlasting Father, Prince of Peace." Isaiah 9:6

This verse contains the first of Isaiah's 25 references to peace. It is an important topic to us. We tease about the typical beauty pageant answer concerning a goal or desire, "World Peace." However, it is bigger than that. We want peace at church, work, school, neighborhood, home, and even within ourselves.

1. Where do you typically struggle to find peace?

_____
_____
_____

Matthew Henry wrote, "Christ died. He left a will in which He gave His soul to His Father, His body to Joseph of Arimathea, His clothes to the soldiers, and His mother to John. But to His disciples, who had left all to follow Him, He left not silver or gold, but something far better - His PEACE!"

Jesus offers peace. Prepositions can be important. We need peace with, from, and of God.

Peace with God

It is crazy to realize, but we are born at war with God. As an infant, we have a sinful nature that encourages us to worship ourselves. We feed that desire throughout life striving to fill a void. That gap can only be filled by Jesus Christ. Yet, we fight the solution. We need and seek peace, but we ignore the **"Prince of Peace."**

Jesus came to earth as a man, lived a perfect life, died for our sins, was buried, and rose again so that we could find peace. We can now have peace with God through Jesus Christ.

John MacArthur said, "God can work peace through us only if He has worked peace in us… Those who are in the best of circumstances but without God can never find peace, but those in the worst of circumstances but with God need never lack peace."

    2. Do you remember what your life was like before you gave your life to Jesus?

_____
_____
_____

C.S. Lewis adds, "God cannot give us a happiness and peace apart from Himself, because it is not there. There is no such thing." We can not have peace from God or the peace of God until we are at peace with God. Jesus is the **"Prince of Peace"** because He made the connection possible.

    3. Do you see the world struggling for peace?

_____
_____
_____

Dwight L. Moody pointed out, "A great many people are trying to make peace, but that has already been done. God has not left it for us to do; all we have to do is to enter into it."

    4. Where does the world strive to find peace aside from Jesus?

_____
_____
_____

    5. What does it mean to enter into the peace of God?

_____
_____
_____

Romans 5:1 gives a great summary for this section, *"Therefore, since we have been justified by faith, we have peace with God through our Lord Jesus Christ."* We have peace with God through the *"Prince of Peace."*

Peace from God

Once you have peace with God, you are open to the blessings that come with peace from God.

6. How is peace from God different than peace with God?
___
___
___

I regularly thought of peace with God (salvation) and peace of God (calmness during the storm) but did not acknowledge peace from God. One of Paul's favorite greetings was a mixture of a Greek and Hebrew blessing, *"Grace to you and peace from God our Father and the Lord Jesus Christ"* (1 Corinthians 1:3). Paul likes to start his letters with this greeting (Romans 1:7; 2 Corinthians 1:2; Galatians 1:3; Ephesians 1:2; Philippians 1:2; Colossians 1:2; 2 Thessalonians 1:2; 1 Timothy 1:2; 2 Timothy 1:2; Titus 1:4; Philemon 1:3). The Greek or Christian greeting emphasized grace while the Hebrew blessing was about peace.

7. Why would peace be such an important part of blessing someone?
___
___
___

There is turmoil in the world. We need peace. Warren Wiersbe said, "Real contentment must come from within. You and I cannot change or control the world around us, but we can change and control the world within us." We must focus on the Lord. We must fix our eyes on Him. Peace comes from Him. He is the *"Prince of Peace."*

I do not know what the future holds, but I know who holds the future!

8. What does this phrase mean to you?

_____
_____
_____

F.B. Meyer gives some very practical advice, "As we pour out our bitterness, God pours in his peace."

9. How can we "pour out our bitterness?"

_____
_____
_____

Peace of God

Philippians 4:7 so beautifully says, **"And the peace of God, which surpasses all understanding, will guard your hearts and your minds in Christ Jesus."** I enjoy reading other translations of the center phrase:

"And the peace of God, which passeth all understanding, shall keep your hearts and minds through Christ Jesus." (KJV)

"And the peace of God, which transcends all understanding, will guard your hearts and your minds in Christ Jesus." (NIV)

The peace of God "passeth, surpasses, and transcends" all understanding. It is hard to explain, and there is no logical explanation outside of the Prince of Peace.

10. What does peace of God mean to you?

_____
_____
_____

11. When have you experienced the peace of God?

_____
_____
_____

In his book, "*Follow Me*", David Platt starts by saying, "I did what everyone expected me to do. I planted a megachurch. I wrote a bestseller. I started a college, planted other churches, and spoke at conferences. But there was a big problem: I lacked peace."

12. Are you so busy "doing" that you are not being still and realizing that He is God?

_____
_____
_____

Isaiah foretold that the **"Prince of Peace"** was coming. Luke 2:14 records a beautiful song that the angels sang at the Savior's birth, **"Glory to God in the highest, and on earth peace among those with whom he is pleased!"** Jesus brought peace and is peace.

Ephesians 2:14 adds, **"For he himself is our peace, who has made us both one and has broken down in his flesh the dividing wall of hostility."** Jesus is our peace.

13. How is Jesus our peace?

_____
_____
_____

14. In his commentary, Robert Jamieson referred to Jesus as "The Tranquillizer." Does this make sense or offend you?

_____
_____
_____

Henry Blackaby admonished, "The Christian needs to walk in peace, so no matter what happens they will be able to bear witness to a watching world." The world knows pain. People can relate to pain, anger, and complaining. They do not understand peace during the storm.

I found an acronym for PEACE that I thought was relevant: People Expressing A Christ Everlasting.

Mother Theresa gave some very basic advice, "Peace begins with a smile."

    15. How can we show peace in the world?
_____
_____
_____

    16. Where do you need to show peace?
_____
_____
_____

"For I know the thoughts that I think toward you, saith the Lord, thoughts of peace, and not of evil, to give you an expected end." Jeremiah 29:11 (KJV)

Notes

Jordan
Devotion #1 - Sierra Combs

A few years ago, my beautiful 22-year-old cousin was killed in a car accident. I wish I had pages of space to tell you her testimony because it is pretty much the most amazing one I have ever witnessed, but perhaps another day. I remember it vividly. Those were some of the most difficult days of my life. On the late October day that she died, I walked into my doctor's office excited for a routine ultrasound of our third baby-to-be, only to find that there was no longer a heartbeat and we had lost the baby. I walked out to my car, and before I even had my seatbelt buckled, my mom called to tell me that Jordan had just been killed. Talk about a double punch in the gut. In the course of 15 minutes, I went from a happy, vibrant girl who was over the moon and excited about the future, to a girl overwhelmed with grief and despair, having just lost two people that I loved. I can still feel the knots in my stomach when I think about that day. I will never forget that funeral. I will never forget the hundreds and hundreds of people who waited in line for hours to pay their respects to the family and say goodbye. I can still see the tear-streamed faces and hear the cries of her friends. This girl touched so many lives. However, the thing I will never forget was her amazingly strong mother and the way she took on that day. She stood for hours, greeting every single person in that line with a huge smile on her face, sharing the Gospel with all of them (several of which accepted Christ by the way; again, another amazing story for another day!). I have never seen anyone exude so much peace as I did that day.

How could a mother who lost her precious daughter just days before have so much peace? How could I find that same source of peace as I mourned the loss of my child, one I would never meet? There was nothing we could do to stop these things – death, loss, wars, sickness, turmoil, and evil. The list seems endless. This world is so chaotic and hard, and we have no control over it. How could anyone ever have peace? Though life's troubles have a way of sneaking up on us, nothing takes God by surprise. Because of His sweet and lovingkindness, He sent us a Savior, the **"Prince of Peace,"** Jesus Christ. However, God never tells us that because we are saved, we will have it easy. He actually tells us the opposite. In John 16:33, Jesus is speaking to His disciples and tells them, **"I have said these things to you, that in me you may have peace. In the world you will have tribulation. But take heart; I have overcome the world."** You see, true peace, God's peace, is not the same as worldly peace. It does not come from a happy life, free from pain and suffering. If it did, no one would ever be able to attain it, at least not for very long. True peace comes from knowing that God is in control. True peace comes from knowing that God is in control and giving that control over to Him (even though it was never even ours to begin with, but hey, it is the thought that counts). God tells us that when we are anxious and troubled that all we have to do is bring that burden to him, **"Come to me, all who labor and are heavy laden, and I will give you rest"** (Matthew 11:28). When we present our requests to God through prayer and petition, then **"the peace of God, which surpasses all understanding, will guard your hearts and your minds in Christ Jesus"** (Philippians 4:7).

As much as I wish that Jordan was still with us and that another little blue-eyed, blonde Combs kid was running around my house, God had a different plan. Sometimes we will not be able to understand the reasons behind the plan, but our God is so faithful and loving. While He does not promise us peace in the way the world would define it, He promises something better. As a child of God, I know that He is in complete control and that no matter what I face in this life, my future is eternally secure. Rest in God's true peace today and every day, giving thanks to the Savior, Jesus Christ, the **"Prince of Peace."**

A Peaceful Season
Devotion #2 - Pastor Philip Piasecki

I am sure when most of us think of the holiday season, we do not think of the word "peace." It seems like Thanksgiving through New Year has become the most insane time of the year. We all have Thanksgiving, Christmas, and New Year's family functions. We all know how interesting it can get when family members get together for Thanksgiving and Christmas. We all can think of that family member combo that will inevitably result in some sort of argument over family history, politics, or some other nonsense! There is also food to make, houses to clean, decorations to put out, lights to put up, presents to buy, Christmas pictures to take, and Christmas cards to send out. Have I successfully raised your blood pressure yet? How does some peace sound?

One of the names of Jesus is **"The Prince of Peace."** That is what Christmas is all about, celebrating the peace that Jesus allows us to have in our lives. We can have peace in relationships, peace with ourselves, peace with our decisions, and the list could go on and on. While all of those things are true and good, they are not even close to as important as one type of peace Jesus brings us.

Ephesians 2:12-14 says, ***"Remember that you were at that time separated from Christ, alienated from the commonwealth of Israel and strangers to the covenants of promise, having no hope and without God in the world. But now in Christ Jesus you who once were far off have been brought near by the blood of Christ. For he himself is our peace, who has made us both one and has broken down in his flesh the dividing wall of hostility."***

Jesus made a way for there to be peace between us and God the Father, God the Son, and God the Holy Spirit. This verse tells us that we were once separated from Christ, had no hope, and were without God. Essentially, we were hopeless. There was no peace between Christ and us; there was strife. That was until Christ, through His blood, brought us near to Him and became our peace. Let the craziness of the holidays be a reminder of the peace that we have through Jesus Christ. That peace can extend through to every aspect of our lives. The **"Prince of Peace"** gave His life for us so that we could have peace between Him and us. I pray that as a church we will focus on the peace that we have through Him and that we would extend that same peace and love to other people. When the world seems crazy around us, rest in the Lord and rest in His peace.

"It is Well with My Soul"
Devotion #3 - Jill Osmon

"For to us a child is born, to us a son is given; and the government shall be upon his shoulder, and his name shall be called Wonderful Counselor, Mighty God, Everlasting Father, Prince of Peace." Isaiah 9:6

Peace seems elusive, even nonexistent, in the world today. As we celebrate this Christmas season, looking at peace, and how God provides it in such a quiet and miraculous way, seems fitting. The holidays can highlight family friction, depression, and overall discontent. We as a church see more phone calls wanting counseling, or simply someone to talk to during this time. Why is this? It is because the world seems the opposite of peace; it is chaotic, scary, and confusing.

I love this verse in Isaiah. It uses these lovely comforting names to describe what Jesus will bring to the world and to us. We have looked at all of them but **"Prince of Peace."** What peace does God offer us through his Son? First, He provides peace between us and God. How can we, imperfect as we are, reconcile the enmity between us and God? We need a peacemaker to come and broker peace, by living a perfect life, dying for our sins, and rising from the dead. Jesus made the way to His Father. That is miraculous!

He also gives us peace in our lives. I love the song, *"It is Well with My Soul."* The lyrics have withstood over the years. Take a minute and read them.

> When peace like a river attendeth my way
> When sorrows like sea billows roll
> Whatever my lot, Thou hast taught me to say
> It is well, it is well with my soul

It is well (it is well)
With my soul (with my soul)
It is well, it is well with my soul

Though Satan should buffet, though trials should come
Let this blest assurance control
That Christ (yes, He has) has regarded my helpless estate
And has shed His own blood for my soul

It is well (it is well)
With my soul (with my soul)
It is well, it is well with my soul

My sin, oh the bliss of this glorious thought (a thought)
My sin, not in part, but the whole (every bit, every bit, all of it)
Is nailed to the cross, and I bear it no more (yes)
Praise the Lord, praise the Lord, O my soul

It is well (it is well)
With my soul (with my soul)
It is well, it is well with my soul

Sing it as well
It is well (it is well)
With my soul (with my soul)
It is well, it is well with my soul

And Lord, haste the day when my faith shall be sight
The clouds be rolled back as a scroll
The trump shall resound, and the Lord shall descend
Even so, it is well with my soul

It is well (it is well)
With my soul (with my soul)
It is well, it is well with my soul

Sing up to Jesus, it is well
It is well (it is well)
With my soul (with my soul)
It is well, it is well with my soul

Peace does not mean life is easy and you do not have to navigate really difficult seasons; but what it means is that "whatever my lot," it is well with my soul. Why? It is because God is in control, and He is faithful and good. He is a **"Wonderful Counselor, Mighty God, Everlasting Father, Prince of Peace."** He is everything we need, in all situations, and that gives me peace. Will you claim that today?

Letters to My Little Ones

Devotion #4 - Pastor Ryan Story

A letter to my children:

There is a concept I would like you to have instilled in your heart. There is a Hebrew word, "Shalom." That is a fancy way to say "peace." In Isaiah chapter 9, Isaiah uses the phrase **"Prince of Peace"** to describe Jesus. The root word for peace translates roughly to peace from completeness. Knowing how to be at peace with the completion of Jesus' work is one of the most amazing types of peace you could ever have. Knowing that in any situation, hardship, adversity, and attack, you can rest assured that Jesus is in control should calm your heart in such a great way. Knowing Jesus brought peace to our relationship with God should calm you during any ordeal.

Do not let yourself live in the area of stress, doubt, or faithlessness. There is nothing of profit there. As I type, I am reminded of a song by Hillsong United called *"Prince of Peace."* It is playing on my headphones. One verse of that song strikes me:

> When fear comes knocking, there You'll be my guard
> When day breeds trouble, there you'll hold my heart
> Come storm or battle, God I know Your peace will meet me there

No matter what the outcome, know that our God is there for us. He protects us and wants us to know He is there for His children.

Peace is not something that comes from anything we can do. Peace can only come from growing in God. Peace is a Fruit of the Spirit, and apart from the Spirit, you will not grow in it. To have peace, you have to have the Spirit, and to get the Spirit inside of you, you must know the Son, who is the Prince of Peace. Children, I want you to have peace that is true but know that you will never have that if you do not know who Jesus is. Jesus is the only one who brings true completeness to our lives.

Endless

Devotion #5 - Pastor John Carter

"For to us a child is born, to us a son is given; and the government shall be upon his shoulder, and his name shall be called Wonderful Counselor, Mighty God, Everlasting Father, Prince of Peace. Of the increase of his government and of peace there will be no end, on the throne of David and over his kingdom, to establish it and to uphold it with justice and with righteousness from this time forth and forevermore. The zeal of the Lord of hosts will do this." Isaiah 9:6-7

The title attributed to the coming Messiah in Isaiah 9:6-7 is attributed to Jesus Christ. The particular title **"Prince of Peace,"** indicates some significant things about Jesus. The title **"Prince"** would have been understood as the future leader of a particular people or group. When Jesus is our Lord, He fulfills that title; He is our leader. In our current world and society, peace might be hard to understand. We for sure see the opposite of peace in a very real and dynamic way with current news. So, we see Jesus' title as the one that will lead a particular group of people and will have peace. Verse 7 of this particular passage in Isaiah states, **"of peace there will be no end."** Consider that Jesus is not only the leader of peace but the one who gives it without end. Wow! How awesome is that?

To know that no matter what trial, difficulty, or life circumstance may arise, our Lord is the Prince of Peace, the one who will give it without end. Maybe you have never considered Jesus Christ as someone that holds this title in your life. Maybe you have held onto something that has kept peace from becoming a reality. May I encourage you to look to Jesus as the holder and giver of peace? He is the One who knows every kind of pain that you may endure today. Philippians 4:6-7 says, **"Do not be anxious about anything, but in everything by prayer and supplication with thanksgiving** *let your requests be made known to God. And the peace of God, which surpasses all understanding, will guard your hearts and your minds in Christ Jesus."*

I want that kind of peace to exist in my life, in my family, and in every aspect! Jesus is the answer to that desire. I hope this short reminder may be an encouragement today to look to Jesus for your peace in the difficulties of everyday life.

Peace and Glory

Devotion #6 - Bryan Fox

Now and then, I will look at comments on news articles regarding tragedies in the world. Whether it is about war or killings, there are usually comments along the line of, "How can a loving God allow this to happen?" Then a terrible shooting takes place in a church building, and people go off the charts trash talking about God, religion, and faith.

I have no answer as to why these things happen other than all things work for the glory of God. His plan is not ours and to pretend to understand in our small brain what His ways are, is quite prideful and arrogant to say the least.

To me, **"Prince of Peace"** means having inner peace with God. The fact that I am a child of His brings me comfort and the basis that I can rationalize the many difficulties I encounter in my life. Jesus did not promise a life without pain, sorrow, or difficulties. So when I face these trials, I look to my faith in Jesus for peace in dealing with them. We were born as an enemy to God through our sin; but because of Jesus' death, burial, and resurrection, we have the hope and security of eternal peace. Because of Jesus' sacrifice, we have been brought back to a relationship of peace with God.

Romans 5:1 says, **"Therefore, since we have been justified by faith, we have peace with God through our Lord Jesus Christ."**

In the meantime, tragedies will continue, there will be sickness, disease and famine, mass shootings, death, and destruction. True world peace will become a reality only after Jesus returns.

Philippians 4:6-7 adds, **"Do not be anxious about anything, but in everything by prayer and supplication with thanksgiving let** *your requests be made known to God. And the peace of God, which surpasses all understanding, will guard your hearts and your minds in Christ Jesus."*

Isaiah 9:1-7

ESV

¹ But there will be no gloom for her who was in anguish. In the former time he brought into contempt the land of Zebulun and the land of Naphtali, but in the latter time he has made glorious the way of the sea, the land beyond the Jordan, Galilee of the nations.

² The people who walked in darkness
 have seen a great light;
those who dwelt in a land of deep darkness,
 on them has light shone.
³ You have multiplied the nation;
 you have increased its joy;
they rejoice before you
 as with joy at the harvest,
 as they are glad when they divide the spoil.
⁴ For the yoke of his burden,
 and the staff for his shoulder,
 the rod of his oppressor,
 you have broken as on the day of Midian.
⁵ For every boot of the tramping warrior in battle tumult
 and every garment rolled in blood
 will be burned as fuel for the fire.
⁶ For to us a child is born,
 to us a son is given;
and the government shall be upon his shoulder,
 and his name shall be called
Wonderful Counselor, Mighty God,
 Everlasting Father, Prince of Peace.
⁷ Of the increase of his government and of peace
 there will be no end,
on the throne of David and over his kingdom,
 to establish it and to uphold it
with justice and with righteousness
 from this time forth and forevermore.
The zeal of the Lord of hosts will do this.

Notes

Worth the Wait

Devotion #1 - Pastor Ryan Story

"Of the increase of his government and of peace there will be no end, on the throne of David and over his kingdom, to establish it and to uphold it with justice and with righteousness from this time forth and forevermore. The zeal of the Lord of hosts will do this." Isaiah 9:7

Did you experience a person who had a hard time waiting for Christmas to arrive? This could have been your young child, a teenager hopeful for a new electronic device, or maybe even a loved one who was eager to give a gift to another. Christmas always brings about a fun and joyful expectation. While we looked at all the names that Jesus would be called, we read the next verse in Isaiah and God's Word tells us the exact peace that Jesus will bring. There will be governmental peace, that has no end, that is upheld by the justice and righteousness of Jesus for all time. While this verse will be perfectly fulfilled in the coming Millennium (if you would like to dig more into the Millennium and all things the book of Revelation, we did just finish a summer-long study), we ought to be comforted to know that in His time, we will all be under the rule of Jesus in a real place where there is no sin competing in our hearts to honor Him.

What about today? We wait like small children for Jesus' return. We really do not have another choice. We cannot speed up time, we cannot force the rapture, and we cannot get a DeLorean, acquire some plutonium, and go forward in time. I will be the first to say waiting is difficult. Waiting becomes even more difficult when you start seeing circumstances around you. For Christmas, we see the wonderment of all that this holiday brings and we get more and more excited the closer we get to the 25th. Sadly, living in a world that is ruled by sin, living in a world that has hurt, pain, brokenness, and heartache, our circumstances are bleak; thus, making our wait exceedingly more difficult.

Have you ever looked at the fallenness of the world and thought, "Is Jesus really in charge?" While Jesus' rule will be perfected in the Millennium, we still are in a place where sinful men rule, and pain is ever present. However, we also live in a world where you see addicts give their life to Christ and rely on His strength to stay clean. We live in a world that sees churches take joy to the unfortunate, not in the name of, "it was nice," but in the name of Jesus Christ. We live in a world where Pastors are about to finish another faithful year serving Jesus and ensuring those who God has placed in their care have grown closer to God.

We live in a world that is broken and the effects of sin are still ever visible. We also live in a world that gives small glimpses of what we are waiting for. We see glimpses of the greatness of Jesus. We see glimpses of peace and justice. While we still must wait for the absolute rule of Christ to come, God gives us our Christmas gift early by showing us exactly what is in store for those who are awaiting His return.

"He who testifies to these things says, 'Surely I am coming soon.' Amen. Come, Lord Jesus." Revelation 22:20

Kingdom Building
Devotion #2 - Jeannie Yates

It can be difficult to navigate the holiday season; especially when you get families together. You are supposed to avoid talking about controversial topics, but there is always that one person that just will not let it go! I saw a meme that said it well, "Mom always said don't discuss religion, politics, or money. Seems as though the fanatics, politicians, and rich people failed to get the memo; they won't stop talking!"

What comes to mind when you hear the word "government"? You immediately think of peace and tranquility, right? No, we usually think of division, arguments, dishonesty, and scandals. This is not anything new. Mankind has been arguing about who was or should be in charge ever since the fall of Adam and Eve in Genesis chapter 3. Kings and rulers can never seem to consistently govern with peace and justice. Only One can shoulder that responsibility. Isaiah 9:6-7 tells us, **"For to us a child is born, to us a son is given; and the government shall be upon his shoulder, and his name shall be called Wonderful Counselor, Mighty God, Everlasting Father, Prince of Peace. Of the increase of his government and of peace there will be no end, on the throne of David and over his kingdom, to establish it and to uphold it with justice and with righteousness from this time forth and forevermore. The zeal of the Lord of hosts will do this."**

In *"The Bible Exposition Commentary,"* Warren Wiersbe writes, "Isaiah 9:6 declares both the humanity ('A Child is born') and the deity ('A Son is given') of the Lord Jesus Christ. The prophet then leaps ahead to the Kingdom Age when Messiah will reign in righteousness and justice from David's throne (Revelation 20). If His name is 'Wonderful,' then there will be nothing dull about His reign!

As Counselor, He has the wisdom to rule justly and as the Mighty God, He has the power to execute His wise plans."

We read more about the reign of the Messiah in Jeremiah 23:5, *"Behold, the days are coming, declares the Lord, when I will raise up for David a righteous Branch, and he shall reign as king and deal wisely, and shall execute justice and righteousness in the land. In his days Judah will be saved, and Israel will dwell securely. And this is the name by which he will be called: 'The Lord is our righteousness.'"* Jeremiah adds *"Our Righteousness"* to the list of titles foretold of Jesus in Isaiah chapter 9.

I long for the day when our wise, just, and righteous King takes His rightful place. I do not know about you, but that sounds like the type of government that we could talk about at the holiday dinner table! Until that day, we are not left in the dark. We are not supposed to sit on the bench and wait; our King has given us the job of Kingdom building. Matthew 28:18-20 (NLT) says, *"Jesus came and told his disciples, 'I have been given all authority in heaven and on earth. Therefore, go and make disciples of all the nations, baptizing them in the name of the Father and the Son and the Holy Spirit. Teach these new disciples to obey all the commands I have given you. And be sure of this: I am with you always, even to the end of the age.'"*

Politics

Devotion #3 - Dr. Randy T. Johnson

"Of the increase of his government and of peace there will be no end, on the throne of David and over his kingdom, to establish it and to uphold it with justice and with righteousness from this time forth and forevermore. The zeal of the Lord of hosts will do this." Isaiah 9:7

In the last 40 years, I have helped develop four Chinese churches in the Greater Detroit area. As a Pastor, my responsibilities have included children's church, student ministry, young adults, and the English gatherings. When I speak during a Chinese gathering, I do have an interpreter with me. It is an exciting ministry.

I try not to get too involved with politics. However, I have one aspect where politics has been encouraging and that involves a local Chinese church. A couple of Chinese professors at Oakland University gave their lives to the Lord. They started inviting Chinese students to their homes for an authentic Chinese dinner. (It is common for there to be Chinese graduate students in our area due to the automotive impact of our area). Without fail, the question would arise, "What makes America great?" They would explain "politics" and our godly heritage. The students would ask how they could take this system back to China and Taiwan. The professors would point out that it is not really a system, but a personal relationship with God through Jesus Christ. Students started getting saved and wanted to learn more. They preferred speaking in Mandarin, so instead of attending English-speaking churches, they started having Bible studies. These Bible studies grew "out of control," so they rented a church and eventually built their own building. This is the purest form of church growth. It is beautiful. It is humorous that God has used "politics" to reach people with the need for the Gospel.

Isaiah 9:7 acknowledges that speaking about politics is not rewarding or encouraging. Peace and justice seem to be all too absent but desired. This verse follows a beautiful description of the Lord, **"For to us a child is born, to us a son is given; and the government shall be upon his shoulder, and his name shall be called Wonderful Counselor, Mighty God, Everlasting Father, Prince of Peace."** It is the Lord who will usher in His Kingdom. He will rule. Those who have given their life to Jesus and follow in His ways will reap the benefits of this new beautiful government. Talking about politics will then be much more fulfilling.

God has blessed America. It is time for America to bless God.

Peace and Order

Devotion #4 - Pastor Roy Townsend

Have you ever stopped to wonder why the Christmas holiday is trademarked by the saying, "Peace on Earth"? While I know this is a quote from Luke 2:14 that reads, **"Glory to God in the highest, and on earth peace among those with whom he is pleased!"** However, when I think of the Christmas holiday, I think of almost anything else. Peace and order are not high on my list of this holiday's attributes.

In Isaiah 9:7, we read, **"Of the increase of his government and of peace there will be no end, on the throne of David and over his kingdom, to establish it and to uphold it with justice and with righteousness from this time forth and forevermore. The zeal of the Lord of hosts will do this."** This verse is also tied to a popular Christmas passage, and it is prophesying and describing the peace and order that will be a hallmark of Christ's Kingdom.

In 1 Corinthians 14:33, we read, **"For God is not a God of confusion but of peace. As in all the churches of the saints."** Commentator Wayne Grudem writes, "Paul says, 'God is not a God of confusion but of peace.' Although 'peace' and 'order' have not traditionally been classified as attributes of God, Paul here indicates another quality that we could think of as a distinct attribute of God." However, it would do us good to remember that these verses speak of **"peace among those with whom he is pleased"** because we all know many people who seem to have no peace. Even if we would like to think that people can have peace at Christmastime, I see a lot of heartache, trouble, confusion, and selfishness. We may need to remember that in Isaiah 48:22 God reveals, **"'There is no peace,' says the Lord, 'for the wicked.'"**

If the world, or we, continue to walk in wickedness, we will have no peace. As Jesus was leaving His disciples, He revealed something in John 14:25-29, *"These things I have spoken to you while I am still with you. But the Helper, the Holy Spirit, whom the Father will send in my name, he will teach you all things and bring to your remembrance all that I have said to you. Peace I leave with you; my peace I give to you. Not as the world gives do I give to you. Let not your hearts be troubled, neither let them be afraid. You heard me say to you, 'I am going away, and I will come to you.' If you loved me, you would have rejoiced, because I am going to the Father, for the Father is greater than I. And now I have told you before it takes place, so that when it does take place you may believe."* For those who have accepted Christ's plan of salvation, He left us the *"Helper, the Holy Spirit,"* who will comfort, guide, direct, and allow us to embrace the peace of God this Christmastime. Remember that Christ said, *"My peace I give to you. Not as the world gives do I give to you."* From there He reminds us to *"let not your hearts be troubled,"* because that is really what celebrating Christmas is all about. It is a recognition of God's plan to redeem the world by sending His Son to be our sacrifice so that we may be at peace with God.

He Is Faithful

Devotion #5 - Gary Wright

I have to admit that I have a hard time trusting people. My friend, Mike, however, is the most trustworthy person that I know. When he tells me he is going to do something, it is done. If he tells me he is going to be somewhere at a certain time, he is there. I totally trust Mike because he has been so faithful to his word.

On Christmas, we celebrate the birth of Jesus. When I look back at Old Testament prophecy and see how many hundreds of prophecies Jesus fulfilled, it really has helped me realize how much we can trust God and His Word.

There are also prophecies written about the second coming of Jesus. One of these prophecies is from Isaiah 9:7, *"Of the increase of his government and of peace there will be no end, on the throne of David and over his kingdom, to establish it and to uphold it with justice and with righteousness from this time forth and forevermore. The zeal of the Lord of hosts will do this."*

Isaiah tells us that Jesus will return again someday, taking His rightful place on the throne of David in Jerusalem, which God promised David in 2 Samuel 7:16, *"And your house and your kingdom shall be made sure forever before me. Your throne shall be established forever."* Jesus will not only reign on David's throne during the Millennium, but forevermore. He will rule in fairness (justice) and will do what is right according to God's standards (righteousness). There will be no war or conflict (peace). I love how the verse ends, *"The zeal of the Lord of hosts will do this."* God will do this from His passionate commitment (zeal). We know we can trust the passionate commitment of God because He always does what He says. Knowing that God always does what He says, not only we can trust Him when it comes to the future, but we can also trust Him and His Word right now.

Here are a few of the many promises that God has made that we can depend on right now:

- God promises salvation to those who believe. Romans 10:9 says, **"Because, if you confess with your mouth that Jesus is Lord and believe in your heart that God raised him from the dead, you will be saved."**
- God promises that as believers our lives have a purpose. Ephesians 2:10 says, **"For we are his workmanship, created in Christ Jesus for good works, which God prepared beforehand, that we should walk in them."**
- God promises comfort in our trials. In 2 Corinthians 1:3, we read, **"Blessed be the God and Father of our Lord Jesus Christ, the Father of mercies and God of all comfort."**

I do not know about you, but I am thankful for a God that keeps His promises. Hebrews 10:23 adds, **"Let us hold fast the confession of our hope without wavering, for he who promised is faithful."**

Chaos at Christmas

Devotion #6 - Pastor Philip Piasecki

One of my favorite Christmas movies of all time is, *"Jingle All The Way."* It stars Arnold Schwarzenegger as a workaholic Dad who tries, at the last second, to find his son the perfect "Turboman" action figure for Christmas. However, as is common with Christmas movies, nothing goes right and most of the movie is just pure chaos. It showcases the chaotic side of the holidays, with people fighting over gifts and trying to fight the crowds to buy everything they need for the perfect Christmas. Unfortunately, when I think of the holiday season, I do not often think of the word peace. However, that is exactly what Jesus was sent from Heaven to bring upon this world.

Isaiah 9:7 says, **"Of the increase of his government and of peace there will be no end, on the throne of David and over his kingdom, to establish it and to uphold it with justice and with righteousness from this time forth and forevermore. The zeal of the Lord of hosts will do this."**

The Israelites were waiting on their king to come and establish His Kingdom. They expected a great ruler to come and conquer the Romans by force and establish a physical kingdom in their land. Instead, Jesus came born as a baby. He arrived in the most innocent way possible. Even though it was not the way God's people were expecting, He still had arrived to establish His Kingdom of peace. We too often are looking for something else in our lives to come and bring us peace.

Too often, I find myself being wrapped up in the chaos of this life instead of finding my peace in Jesus. This Scripture teaches us that His peace will increase and of it, **"there will be no end!"** I do not know about you, but personally, I desire the never-ending peace that only Jesus can offer. We have to understand that the gift that

Jesus offers us is so much better than anything that the world can offer us. Around Christmas, we not only have a better opportunity to recognize this gift, but also a better opportunity than normal to share the truth of that gift with those around us. When you see someone who is just being lost in the chaos of this world, do not hesitate to share with them the peace that Jesus offers through His Gospel.

OUR VISION

Matthew 28:19-20: *"Go therefore and make disciples of all nations, baptizing them in the name of the Father and of the Son and of the Holy Spirit, teaching them to observe all that I have commanded you. And behold, I am with you always, to the end of the age."*

REACH

At The River Church, you will often hear the phrase, "We don't go to church, we are the Church." We believe that as God's people, our primary purpose and goal is to go out and make disciples of Jesus Christ. We encourage you to reach the world in your local communities.

GATHER

The goal of weekend gatherings at The River Church is to glorify Christ in all we do! Whether it be through singing, giving, serving, or any of the variety of ways He has gifted us and called us together, Jesus is at the center of it all. We celebrate that when followers of Christ gather together in unity, it's not only a refresher, it brings life-change!

GROW

Our Growth Communities are designed to mirror the early church in Acts as having *"all things in common."* They are smaller collections of believers who spend time together studying the Word, knowing and caring for one another relationally, and learning to increase their commitment to Christ by holding one another accountable.

The River Church
8393 E. Holly Rd.
Holly, MI 48442

theriverchurch.cc • info@theriverchurch.cc